Technology Use Is Not Enough

Students are changing...

"We don't have to wait until we're grown up to work together internationally. We can do it right now. Kids already know how to use the tools; we just need the teachers to set up the projects and let us go!"

Chloe, Charlottesville, VA,
Grade 6, Age 11

Society is changing...

"Every young person will need to use ICT (Information and Communication Technology) in many different ways in their adult lives, in order to participate fully in a modern society."

Are Students Ready for a Technology-Rich World? Organisation for Economic Co-operation and Development (OECD, 2006)

Our world is changing...

"We've progressed from a society of farmers to a society of factory workers to a society of knowledge workers. And now we're progressing yet again— to a society of creators and empathizers, of pattern recognizers and meaning makers."

A Whole New Mind,
Daniel H. Pink (2006)

Education must change...

We are reminded at the release of each new report on workplace readiness and the emerging global economy that foundational technology skills—especially competence with information and communication technologies (ICT)—are increasingly important for our students preparing to work, live, and contribute to the social and civic fabric of their communities. What we have learned in the two decades of dramatically increasing penetration of these technologies into our society is that these foundational ICT skills are not sufficient. As with other basic skills, we know that unless students are given the opportunity and charged with the expectation to *apply these basics* in authentic, integrated ways to solve problems, complete projects, and creatively extend their abilities, then mastering these basics will not really make much difference in the long run. So, although basic skills, concepts, and knowledge are prerequisite to fully participating in society as our young learners become adults, they do not sufficiently equip future workers, leaders, and contributing global citizens.

For that reason, the ISTE National Educational Technology Standards for Students (NETS•S) identify several higher order skills and digital citizenship as critical if we are to truly provide students the opportunity to learn effectively for a lifetime and live productively in our emerging global society and increasingly digital world.

Supporting a New Generation of Technology Standards

Rapid advances in technology affect every facet of our lives, from the way we conduct business to the social relationships we form. With globally distributed workforces, communication systems, and infrastructures, even the least technologically or economically developed nations are able to experience at least some of the benefits. As the economic and social landscape changes, demands on educators and students shift as well. Although traditional literacy skills are still important, students must master a host of new skills in order to become successful global citizens. The refreshed ISTE NETS•S provide a framework for educators to use as they transition schools from Industrial Age to Digital Age places of learning.

This shift requires more than access to technology or references to technology use in content area standards. Certain systemic conditions are necessary for schools to effectively use ICT for learning, teaching, and educational management. Physical, human, financial, and policy decisions greatly affect the implementation of authentic learning opportunies and environments conducive to creativeness, innovation, and global awareness.

Several essential conditions are required to create learning environments conducive to powerful uses of technology and digital learning resources.

"A critical factor in the effective use of ICT is the existence of a school-level e-strategy that addresses future development and sustainability and includes some means of monitoring progress against identified milestones."

The Impact of ICT in Schools— A Landscape Review, British Educational Communications and Technology Agency (Becta, 2007)

"Technology integration is occurring if:

▸ teachers are trained in a full range of technology uses and in the determination of their appropriate roles and applications;

▸ teachers and students routinely turn to technology when needed; and

▸ teachers and students are empowered and supported in carrying out those choices.

Under these conditions, the potential of digital technologies to improve teaching and learning is likely to be realized."

Overview of Technology Integration, Northwest Educational Technology Consortium (NETC, 2005)

Essential Conditions

Necessary conditions to effectively leverage technology for learning

Shared Vision
Proactive leadership in developing a shared vision for educational technology among school personnel, students, parents, and the community

Implementation Planning
A systemic plan aligned with a shared vision for school effectiveness and student learning through the infusion of ICT and digital learning resources

Consistent and Adequate Funding
Ongoing funding to support technology infrastructure, personnel, digital resources, and staff development

Equitable Access
Robust and reliable access to current and emerging technologies and digital resources, with connectivity for all students, teachers, staff, and school leaders

Skilled Personnel
Educators and support staff skilled in the use of ICT appropriate for their job responsibilities

Ongoing Professional Learning
Technology-related professional learning plans and opportunities with dedicated time to practice and share ideas

Technical Support
Consistent and reliable assistance for maintaining, renewing, and using ICT and digital resources

Curriculum Framework
Content standards and related digital curriculum resources

Student-Centered Learning
Use of ICT to facilitate engaging approaches to learning

Assessment and Evaluation
Continuous assessment, both of learning and for learning, and evaluation of the use of ICT and digital resources

Engaged Communities
Partnerships and collaboration within the community to support and fund the use of ICT and digital resources

Support Policies
Policies, financial plans, accountability measures, and incentive structures to support the use of ICT in learning and in district and school operations

Supportive External Context
Policies and initiatives at the national, regional, and local levels to support schools in the effective implementation of technology for achieving curriculum and technology (ICT) standards

NETS Project Overview

The Challenge

The challenge facing schools worldwide is to empower all students to function effectively now and in a future marked by increasing change, evolving technologies, and the phenomenal growth of information.

The Potential

Technology is a powerful tool with enormous potential for providing learning opportunities that will serve the needs of today's students throughout their lifetimes.

The Goal

Through the NETS Project, ISTE encourages educational leaders to use technology (ICT) standards to provide environments that enable students to use technology for improved learning. This includes assisting educational leaders in recognizing and addressing the essential conditions (see p. 3) for the effective use of technology in school settings.

The Results

Since the ISTE NETS•S were released in 1998, they have been widely used to set educational technology expectations for students in schools across America and around the globe. The 1998 student standards were a springboard for NETS for Teachers (2000) and NETS for Administrators (2002). The NETS Project has also provided teachers, technology planners, teacher preparation institutions, and educational decision makers with a wide variety of additional standards-based resources for establishing enriched learning environments supported by technology.

The Refresh Process

ISTE remains committed to tapping the collective wisdom of the global educational technology community for fresh and meaningful guidance and leadership. The goal for this first refresh of the NETS•S was to collect input from a variety of stakeholders through a series of events designed to solicit as much feedback as possible. The process included open forums at major education conferences and meetings; focus groups to collect input from education, business, and community organizations; and online surveys. The ISTE Accreditation and Standards Committee compiled the responses and developed a draft that was reviewed and revised by the ISTE Stakeholders Advisory Council. The resulting draft of the refreshed NETS•S was then submitted for additional comments and suggestions online and in open forums. The NETS•S were adopted by the ISTE Board of Directors on May 4, 2007.

Then and Now
The ISTE NETS for Students

1998

Basic Operations and Concepts

Social, Ethical, and Human Issues

Technology Productivity Tools

Technology Communications Tools

Technology Research Tools

Technology Problem Solving and Decision Making Tools

2007

Creativity and Innovation

Communication and Collaboration

Research and Information Fluency

Critical Thinking, Problem Solving,
and Decision Making

Digital Citizenship

Technology Operations and Concepts

Adapting the Refreshed NETS•S for Global Use

Regardless of where you live, advances in technology are having an effect on your life. In places where simple access is still a burning issue, you are probably trying to identify ways to develop and launch a reliable infrastructure so that students may begin mastering basic technology skills. In places where infrastructure is no longer a concern, you are most likely grappling with how to give your students a competitive edge in this new global society. In any case, the NETS•S may be adapted to help meet your educational needs. Here are a few steps you can take to get started:

1. Secure the support of essential stakeholders.

2. If you don't have existing technology (ICT) standards and technology is not incorporated into your content standards, use the ISTE NETS•S as a foundation.

3. If you already have national technology standards or content standards that incorporate technology, compare them with the ISTE NETS•S to identify gaps.

4. Review your content standards to identify opportunies for integration with ISTE NET•S or to determine if all the NETS•S have been addressed.

5. Review the international scenarios found in the Profiles section of this booklet and gather your own examples of exemplary technology use.

6. Use local experts from within your own community or country who support instructional technology use.

7. When it is time to localize the ISTE NETS•S, you will need adequate resources to:

   a. obtain accurate translations of the standards and profiles,

   b. put them into the context of your culture, and

   c. address the needs of your teachers and students.

The World Has Changed and So Must We

Although the original NETS•S identified skills and knowledge every student needed to succeed in the technology and information environment that was emerging in 1998, the spotlight was on the tools themselves. In contrast, these new student standards focus on skills and knowledge that students need to learn effectively and live productively in an increasingly digital society. The emphasis now is on cognitive and learning skills, as well as on creativity and innovation. The presentation order of the standards has also changed, with a shift away from competency with technology tools to technology (ICT) use that focuses on skills required in a digital world to learn, plan, produce, and innovate.

As educators apply these refreshed standards, they will find that existing standards-based resources retain their value. Students still need to learn "the basics." However, we need to expand and enhance these resources to take advantage of the capabilities of new and evolving technologies. ISTE maintains its commitment to providing new and updated resources to assist teachers in making this transition.

The world has changed, and so must we. The following chart lists characteristics representing traditional approaches to learning and corresponding strategies often associated with new learning environments.

Transforming Learning Environments with **Technology**

Technology-Enabled Strategies for Student Learning

Traditional Environments	→	Emerging Learning Landscape
Teacher-directed, memory-focused instruction	→	Student-centered, performance-focused learning
Lockstep, prescribed-path progression	→	Flexible progression with multipath options
Limited media, single-sense stimulation	→	Media-rich, multisensory stimulation
Knowledge from limited, authoritative sources	→	Learner-constructed knowledge from multiple information sources and experiences
Isolated work on invented exercises	→	Collaborative work on authentic, real-world projects
Mastery of fixed content and specified processes	→	Student engagement in definition, design, and management of projects
Factual, literal thinking for competence	→	Creative thinking for innovation and original solutions
In-school expertise, content, and activities	→	Global expertise, information, and learning experiences
Stand-alone communication and information tools	→	Converging information and communication systems
Traditional literacy and communication skills	→	Digital literacies and communication skills
Primary focus on school and local community	→	Expanded focus including digital global citizenship
Isolated assessment of learning	→	Integrated assessment for learning

Information and Communication Technology (ICT) Standards for All Students

Traditional educational practices no longer provide students with all the necessary skills for economic survival in today's workplace. Students must now apply strategies for solving problems using appropriate tools for learning, researching, collaborating, and communicating. The ISTE NETS Refresh Project is designed to provide teachers, technology and curriculum planners, teacher educators, and educational decision makers with frameworks, standards, and performance indicators to guide them in establishing enriched learning environments supported by technology. These new learning environments provide rich opportunities for students to find and use current information and resources, and apply academic skills for solving real-world problems. These environments engage students in activities that interweave educational technology skills and relevant curricular content.

The refreshed technology (ICT) standards for all students are organized into six categories, each expanded by a broad standard statement and more descriptive performance indicators that represent current best practice in both student technology use and Digital-Age learning skills. These standards and performance indicators are designed to be introduced and reinforced over time, until students achieve mastery. The profiles for technology (ICT) literate students (see pp. 10–23) include sample learning activities that link back to the six standards and provide teachers examples to use when planning developmentally appropriate technology-supported activities. It is important to remember that the technology standards for all students are a guide, not a mandate. Also, educators will need to adapt the standards to meet local needs, depending upon how and to what degree the factors described in the essential conditions (see p. 3) provide the necessary environment.

Definitions

ICT stands for information and communication technology. This acronym is used throughout much of the world in place of the word *technology* when referring to skills or standards for technology use.

Educational technology refers to the application of technology skills for learning.

Technology use has evolved, and so have the ISTE NETS for Students.

What students should know and be able to do to learn effectively and live productively in an increasingly digital world…

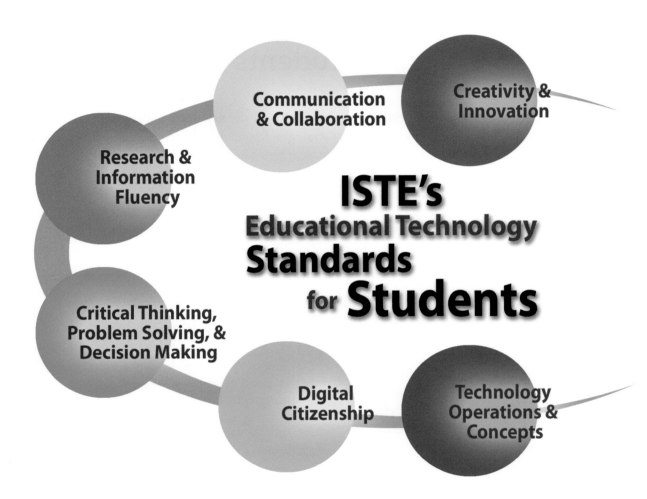

NETS•S Organization

The technology standards for students are divided into six broad categories. A brief standard statement follows each category. The four performance indicators (a–d) for each standard provide specific outcomes to be measured. The Profiles for Technology Literate Students (see pp. 10–23) provide examples of student performances at various ages and grade levels.

The ISTE
National Educational Technology Standards (NETS•S) and Performance Indicators for Students

1. **Creativity and Innovation**
   Students demonstrate creative thinking, construct knowledge, and develop innovative products and processes using technology. Students:
   a. apply existing knowledge to generate new ideas, products, or processes.
   b. create original works as a means of personal or group expression.
   c. use models and simulations to explore complex systems and issues.
   d. identify trends and forecast possibilities.

2. **Communication and Collaboration**
   Students use digital media and environments to communicate and work collaboratively, including at a distance, to support individual learning and contribute to the learning of others. Students:
   a. interact, collaborate, and publish with peers, experts, or others employing a variety of digital environments and media.
   b. communicate information and ideas effectively to multiple audiences using a variety of media and formats.
   c. develop cultural understanding and global awareness by engaging with learners of other cultures.
   d. contribute to project teams to produce original works or solve problems.

3. **Research and Information Fluency**
   Students apply digital tools to gather, evaluate, and use information. Students:
   a. plan strategies to guide inquiry.
   b. locate, organize, analyze, evaluate, synthesize, and ethically use information from a variety of sources and media.
   c. evaluate and select information sources and digital tools based on the appropriateness to specific tasks.
   d. process data and report results.

4. **Critical Thinking, Problem Solving, and Decision Making**
   Students use critical thinking skills to plan and conduct research, manage projects, solve problems, and make informed decisions using appropriate digital tools and resources. Students:
   a. identify and define authentic problems and significant questions for investigation.
   b. plan and manage activities to develop a solution or complete a project.
   c. collect and analyze data to identify solutions and/or make informed decisions.
   d. use multiple processes and diverse perspectives to explore alternative solutions.

5. **Digital Citizenship**
   Students understand human, cultural, and societal issues related to technology and practice legal and ethical behavior. Students:
   a. advocate and practice safe, legal, and responsible use of information and technology.
   b. exhibit a positive attitude toward using technology that supports collaboration, learning, and productivity.
   c. demonstrate personal responsibility for lifelong learning.
   d. exhibit leadership for digital citizenship.

6. **Technology Operations and Concepts**
   Students demonstrate a sound understanding of technology concepts, systems, and operations. Students:
   a. understand and use technology systems.
   b. select and use applications effectively and productively.
   c. troubleshoot systems and applications.
   d. transfer current knowledge to learning of new technologies.

Profiles

for Technology (ICT) Literate Students

A major component of the NETS Project is the development of a general set of profiles describing technology (ICT) literate students at key developmental points in their precollege education. These profiles are based on ISTE's core belief that all students must have regular opportunities to use technology to develop skills that encourage personal productivity, creativity, critical thinking, and collaboration in the classroom and in daily life. Coupled with the standards, the profiles provide a set of examples for preparing students to be lifelong learners and contributing members of a global society.

The profiles highlight a few important types of learning activities in which students might engage as the new NETS•S are implemented. These examples are provided in an effort to bring the standards to life and demonstrate the variety of activities possible. Space limitations and the realities of the constantly evolving learning and technology landscapes make it impossible to provide a comprehensive collection of examples in this document, and consequently, students and teachers should not feel constrained by this resource. Similarly, because this represents only a sampling of illuminating possibilities, the profiles cannot be considered a comprehensive curriculum, or even a minimally adequate one, for achieving mastery of the rich revised National Educational Technology Standards for Students. Educators are encouraged to stay connected to the ISTE NETS Refresh Project and contribute their best examples to expand this resource.

The profiles are divided into the following four grade ranges. Because grade-level designations vary in different countries, age ranges are also provided.

> ▶ Grades PK–2 (ages 4–8)
>
> ▶ Grades 3–5 (ages 8–11)
>
> ▶ Grades 6–8 (ages 11–14)
>
> ▶ Grades 9–12 (ages 14–18)

It's important to remember that the profiles are *indicators of achievement at certain stages* in primary, elementary, and secondary education, and that success in meeting the indicators is predicated on students having regular access to a variety of technology tools. Skills are introduced and reinforced over multiple grade levels before mastery is achieved. If access is an issue, profile indicators will need to be adapted to fit local needs.

The standards and profiles are based on input and feedback provided by instructional technology experts and educators from around the world, including classroom teachers, administrators, teacher educators, and curriculum specialists. Students were also given opportunities to provide input and feedback. In addition, these refreshed documents reflect information collected from professional literature.

Technology Implementation—

Scenarios

In addition to a list of example learning activities, each profile is illustrated with two authentic scenarios that relate exemplary ways students are using technology to increase skills and expand or enhance their learning in the classroom. These scenarios describe activities that reflect not only the NETS•S, but also relevant curriculum standards—underscoring an ISTE core belief that technology use should not occur in isolation, but as an integral part of learning across all skills and subject areas. These scenarios depict promising practices from around the globe.

Profile

for Technology (ICT) Literate Students
Grades PK–2 (Ages 4–8)

The following experiences with technology and digital resources are examples of learning activities in which students might engage during PK–Grade 2 (ages 4–8):

1. Illustrate and communicate original ideas and stories using digital tools and media-rich resources. (1, 2)

2. Identify, research, and collect data on an environmental issue using digital resources and propose a developmentally appropriate solution. (1, 3, 4)

3. Engage in learning activities with learners from multiple cultures through e-mail and other electronic means. (2, 6)

4. In a collaborative work group, use a variety of technologies to produce a digital presentation or product in a curriculum area. (1, 2, 6)

5. Find and evaluate information related to a current or historical person or event using digital resources. (3)

6. Use simulations and graphical organizers to explore and depict patterns of growth such as the life cycles of plants and animals. (1, 3, 4)

7. Demonstrate the safe and cooperative use of technology. (5)

8. Independently apply digital tools and resources to address a variety of tasks and problems. (4, 6)

9. Communicate about technology using developmentally appropriate and accurate terminology. (6)

10. Demonstrate the ability to navigate in virtual environments such as electronic books, simulation software, and Web sites. (6)

The numbers in parentheses after each item identify the standards (1–6) most closely linked to the activity described. Each activity may relate to one indicator, to multiple indicators, or to the overall standards referenced.

The categories are:

1. Creativity and Innovation
2. Communication and Collaboration
3. Research and Information Fluency
4. Critical Thinking, Problem Solving, and Decision Making
5. Digital Citizenship
6. Technology Operations and Concepts

Scenarios Grades PK–2 (Ages 4–8)

Scenario 1

Heat Energy

Grade Level: 2

Technology Standards: 1, 2, 3, 4, 6

Content Areas: Science, Mathematics

Teacher: Meg Griffin

School: Cold Spring Elementary School

Location: Doylestown, Pennsylvania, United States

Second-grade teacher Meg Griffin helps her students learn about scientific inquiry using technology. While studying energy concepts, her students use electronic temperature probes to explore heat energy. Students begin by using the probes to measure and record the temperature of their hands. Following a discussion of ways they might increase or decrease their hand temperature, students try out their ideas using the probes to measure. Based on the results, students draw conclusions about which strategies resulted in temperature changes.

From hand temperature, Griffin's students move to explorations of water temperature and the effect that insulators have on the temperature of liquids. Students use the probes to collect temperature data from jars of water ranging from cold to hot, and then categorize the data along a gradient. Next, students work together to investigate the effects of various insulators (e.g., paper towels, aluminum foil) on temperature. Probes are used to gather data and generate charts to compare results.

Finally, students are challenged to use the knowledge they have gained about temperature and insulators to find a way to keep hot beverages hot. Working in teams, students design and create a heat saver. After reviewing data for each team, students decide which design was most successful in limiting heat loss.

Not only do students grasp abstract concepts related to heat energy, they also are actively engaged in learning and applying that learning to solve a real-world problem.

Scenarios Grades PK–2 (Ages 4–8)

Scenario 2

Retell Me a Story

Grade Levels: 1–2

Technology Standards: 1, 2, 6

Content Area: Language Arts

Teacher-Librarian: Suzanne Vanderpool

School: Mossman State School

Location: Mossman, Queensland, Australia

One of the best ways to help young students master reading skills such as vocabulary, sequencing, characterization, and plot line is to have them retell familiar stories. When primary-age students visit the school library at Mossman State School, teacher-librarian Suzanne Vanderpool takes this idea a step further by engaging students in retelling animated fairy tales using a digital paint program and presentation software.

After viewing a sample animated fairy tale, students are divided into working groups of up to eight members. Once they've selected the fairy tale they will retell, they make a list of the characters and settings in the story, which Vanderpool saves as a word processing document for later use. Then each student selects one or more characters or settings to draw, using the digital paint program. Vanderpool imports the students' drawings into a digital photo editor so they can be easily added to digital presentation slides.

Next, the students and Vanderpool walk through the process of inserting the drawings onto presentation slides and adding animations. Although she does most of the actual graphics manipulation, students are actively engaged in discussing the steps involved and deciding where each drawing should be placed. By the end of this activity, students are taking turns completing simple insertion or animation tasks. Once the slides and animations are completed, text boxes and text are added to each slide, again with student input.

In the culminating activity, each group shares its animated fairy tale with the rest of the class. The files are kept as a resource for other classes. This project has been so successful with younger students that Vanderpool now uses their files as samples for older students (ages 11–12) who are retelling stories on their own.

Profile
for Technology (ICT) Literate Students
Grades 3–5 (Ages 8–11)

The following experiences with technology and digital resources are examples of learning activities in which students might engage during Grades 3–5 (ages 8–11):

1. Produce a media-rich digital story about a significant local event based on first-person interviews. (1, 2, 3, 4)

2. Use digital-imaging technology to modify or create works of art for use in a digital presentation. (1, 2, 6)

3. Recognize bias in digital resources while researching an environmental issue with guidance from the teacher. (3, 4)

4. Select and apply digital tools to collect, organize, and analyze data to evaluate theories or test hypotheses. (3, 4, 6)

5. Identify and investigate a global issue and generate possible solutions using digital tools and resources. (3, 4)

6. Conduct science experiments using digital instruments and measurement devices. (4, 6)

7. Conceptualize, guide, and manage individual or group learning projects using digital planning tools with teacher support. (4, 6)

8. Practice injury prevention by applying a variety of ergonomic strategies when using technology. (5)

9. Debate the effect of existing and emerging technologies on individuals, society, and the global community. (5, 6)

10. Apply previous knowledge of digital technology operations to analyze and solve current hardware and software problems. (4, 6)

The numbers in parentheses after each item identify the standards (1–6) most closely linked to the activity described. Each activity may relate to one indicator, to multiple indicators, or to the overall standards referenced.

The categories are:

1. Creativity and Innovation
2. Communication and Collaboration
3. Research and Information Fluency
4. Critical Thinking, Problem Solving, and Decision Making
5. Digital Citizenship
6. Technology Operations and Concepts

Scenarios Grades 3–5 (Ages 8–11)

Scenario 1

Project Puffin

Grade Level: 3

Technology Standards: 2, 3, 6

Content Areas: Science, Language Arts

Teacher: Cathy Evanoff

School: Nags Head Elementary School

Location: Nags Head, North Carolina, United States

On a chilly January day in North Carolina, four third-grade classes and their teachers travel 805 miles, in less than a minute, to the Gulf of Maine to interview Susan Schubel of the National Audubon Society's Project Puffin. Previously, the students read Bruce McMillan's story *Night of the Pufflings* and extended the story by conducting a mini-research project about these amazing little birds. During their online research, the students learned that the National Audubon Society started Project Puffin in 1973 to learn how to restore puffins to historic nesting islands in the Gulf of Maine. And now, placing a call using Voice over Internet Protocol (VoIP), the children speak directly with the "Bird Lady" to learn more about the project and real-life puffin experiences.

The opportunity to interview an outreach educator for the Puffin Project engages even the most reluctant students. Prior to the interview, students develop questions based upon the material they read. During the interview, Schubel provides background information about herself and Project Puffin and then answers the questions the students pose. Photos of this exciting event and a podcast of the highlights of the interview are then made available online.

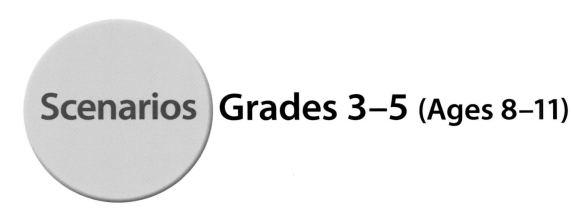

Scenarios Grades 3–5 (Ages 8–11)

Scenario 2

Videoconferencing for Student and Teacher Learning

Grade Level: 4

Technology Standards: 2, 5, 6

Content Area: Foreign Language

Teachers: Lorine Sweeney and Deb Venance

School: Buffalo Trail Public Schools

Location: Wainwright, Alberta, Canada

Technology in Education Is Global

Year 6 students (ages 10–11) at Usk Church in Wales Primary School (Monmouthshire, Wales, UK) begin to grasp the size of our solar system by studying the length of time it takes the planets to orbit the sun one time. Using a simple spreadsheet created by Deputy Headteacher Stuart Ball, students discover what their current age would be on another planet and use that concrete reference point to engage in conversations about larger, more abstract ideas about the solar system.

Buffalo Trail Public Schools, a district in rural Alberta, Canada, is using innovative videoconferencing technology to expand the number of students taking French as a second language. At the same time, teacher capacity is being built by developing district teachers' second language skills.

The challenge? The district, which covers approximately 14,000 square kilometers, was asked by provincial legislators to provide French as a second language instruction to every Grade 4 student in 15 schools. The problem was that only five district teachers were confident in second-language pedagogy, and 10 schools did not offer French language instruction at all. The solution? The board hired one full-time master teacher, who created lessons and resources for a full year of Grade 4 French. Then, with the resources and equipment in place at the 10 receiving schools, the master teacher used videoconferencing to convey the lessons to the students and their teachers.

The students love learning through videoconferencing, vying for turns using the interactive white board and engaging in activities with other students as much as 100 miles away. They also witness their teachers in the role of learners. A high point of the first year took place when the provincial minister of education visited classes by videoconferencing. Now in its third year, the French as a second language program in this district has 17 teachers who have not only gained proficiency in teaching French, but also have (along with students, parents, and board members) learned about the positive power of technology in teaching and learning.

Profile

for Technology (ICT) Literate Students
Grades 6–8 (Ages 11–14)

The following experiences with technology and digital resources are examples of learning activities in which students might engage during Grades 6–8 (ages 11–14):

1. Describe and illustrate a content-related concept or process using a model, simulation, or concept-mapping software. (1, 2)

2. Create original animations or videos documenting school, community, or local events. (1, 2, 6)

3. Gather data, examine patterns, and apply information for decision making using digital tools and resources. (1, 4)

4. Participate in a cooperative learning project in an online learning community. (2)

5. Evaluate digital resources to determine the credibility of the author and publisher and the timeliness and accuracy of the content. (3)

6. Employ data-collection technology such as probes, handheld devices, and geographic mapping systems to gather, view, analyze, and report results for content-related problems. (3, 4, 6)

7. Select and use the appropriate tools and digital resources to accomplish a variety of tasks and to solve problems. (3, 4, 6)

8. Use collaborative electronic authoring tools to explore common curriculum content from multicultural perspectives with other learners. (2, 3, 4, 5)

9. Integrate a variety of file types to create and illustrate a document or presentation. (1, 6)

10. Independently develop and apply strategies for identifying and solving routine hardware and software problems. (4, 6)

The numbers in parentheses after each item identify the standards (1–6) most closely linked to the activity described. Each activity may relate to one indicator, to multiple indicators, or to the overall standards referenced.

The categories are:

1. Creativity and Innovation
2. Communication and Collaboration
3. Research and Information Fluency
4. Critical Thinking, Problem Solving, and Decision Making
5. Digital Citizenship
6. Technology Operations and Concepts

Scenarios Grades 6–8 (Ages 11–14)

Scenario 1

Coming to Texas

Grade Level: 7

Technology Standards: 1, 2, 3, 4, 6

Content Area: Social Studies

Teacher: Mark McCall

School: Stephen F. Austin Middle School

Location: Bryan, Texas, United States

Why were U.S. citizens willing to migrate to empresario colonies in Texas during the 1820s? Social studies teacher Mark McCall poses this question to his seventh-grade students at Stephen F. Austin Middle School each year. And now that the school has a 1-to-1 student-to-laptop computer ratio, students use the technology to discover, evaluate, and synthesize information, and to share their learning in a dynamic environment that brings real-world problem-solving skills into the classroom.

To find the answer to McCall's question, students form research teams and are assigned a specific colony. They use their laptops to access a wiki created by McCall (housed on the school's local course management system) that contains background material about the empresario colonies. Students create a mind map with concept-mapping software to organize the information they find. Next, each research team uses its mind map to identify key points about the team's assigned colony and then creates a poster highlighting the unique benefits of that colony. Posters are presented during a "learning walk," in which students compare, contrast, and evaluate key information on each poster.

Some teachers might end the unit at this point, but not McCall. After the learning walk, students form new teams to script and record a modern-day radio commercial to market the Texas colonies to one of four target audiences in the U.S. or Mexico. Students use music editing and digital media player software to produce a class podcast of Texas commercials.

This final task challenges students to take the information learned in the poster activity, synthesize those ideas, and then demonstrate their learning by working collaboratively to create a new product.

Scenarios Grades 6–8 (Ages 11–14)

Scenario 2

Courage Against All Odds

Grade Levels: 7–8

Technology Standards: 1, 2, 3, 4, 6

Content Areas: History, Language Arts

Teacher: Chrysanthi Palazi

School: 3rd Junior High

Location: Serres, Greece

Technology in Education Is Global

Middle school students (ages 11–14) at St. Elisabeth's School (Van Nuys, California) learn to see the world through the eyes of other students in countries including Belgium, Scotland, and New Zealand through the Photo-a-Day for Schools project, spearheaded by Principal Barbara Barreda and hosted on Flickr.

The Battle of Thermopylae, which took place in 480 BC, is a classic example of courage against all odds. Vastly outnumbered and facing certain death, 300 Spartan soldiers held off an invading Persian army long enough for Greek troops in Athens to prepare for a naval battle that turned the tide of the war. Junior high students in Greece study this event using the book *Historiae* (*The Histories*) written by the ancient historian Herodotus. Teacher Chrysanthi Palazi makes this unit of study more accessible to her students by integrating the use of the Internet and presentation software to assist students in creating a project that demonstrates their understanding of the original event and draws parallels to modern life.

Palazi divides the class into four study groups. Each group is responsible for researching and making a presentation about the group's area of study. The first group focuses on historical texts written by various authors to share factual information about the battle. The second group identifies archaeological remains and creates a virtual display of the location, weaponry, and other pertinent details. This group also explores strategies used by both armies during the battle. The third group makes a collection of links to poetry, songs, books, and other artifacts inspired by the bravery of the Spartan soldiers. The fourth group analyzes several recent movies based on (or inspired by) this battle and explores the legacy of this event in modern Greece.

At the conclusion of the project, students have created a comprehensive study guide that includes text, pictures, video clips, and links to Web-based resources, all easily accessible through hyperlinked presentation slides.

Profile
for Technology (ICT) Literate Students
Grades 9–12 (Ages 14–18)

The following experiences with technology and digital resources are examples of learning activities in which students might engage during Grades 9–12 (ages 14–18):

1. Design, develop, and test a digital learning game to demonstrate knowledge and skills related to curriculum content. (1, 4)

2. Create and publish an online art gallery with examples and commentary that demonstrate an understanding of different historical periods, cultures, and countries. (1, 2)

3. Select digital tools or resources to use for a real-world task and justify the selection based on their efficiency and effectiveness. (3, 6)

4. Employ curriculum-specific simulations to practice critical-thinking processes. (1, 4)

5. Identify a complex global issue, develop a systematic plan of investigation, and present innovative sustainable solutions. (1, 2, 3, 4)

6. Analyze the capabilities and limitations of current and emerging technology resources and assess their potential to address personal, social, lifelong learning, and career needs. (4, 5, 6)

7. Design a Web site that meets accessibility requirements. (1, 5)

8. Model legal and ethical behaviors when using information and technology by properly selecting, acquiring, and citing resources. (3, 5)

9. Create media-rich presentations for other students on the appropriate and ethical use of digital tools and resources. (1, 5)

10. Configure and troubleshoot hardware, software, and network systems to optimize their use for learning and productivity. (4, 6)

The numbers in parentheses after each item identify the standards (1–6) most closely linked to the activity described. Each activity may relate to one indicator, to multiple indicators, or to the overall standards referenced.

The categories are:

1. Creativity and Innovation
2. Communication and Collaboration
3. Research and Information Fluency
4. Critical Thinking, Problem Solving, and Decision Making
5. Digital Citizenship
6. Technology Operations and Concepts

Scenarios Grades 9–12 (Ages 14–18)

Scenario 1

Brought to You Live from Park City High School!

Grade Levels: 9–12

Technology Standards: 1, 2, 3, 4, 6

Content Areas: Language Arts, Visual and Performing Arts

Teacher: Christopher S. Maddux

School: Park City High School

Location: Park City, Utah, United States

Presenting a live, daily television broadcast to more than 1,200 peers and 80 adults may seem like a daunting task, but that's exactly what Christopher Maddux's high school students accomplish five times per week! Every school day, students prepare an 11-minute live television program that focuses on school news and events, and then broadcast it throughout the campus. Students take responsibility for finding talent, writing scripts, operating the cameras, directing or producing segments, designing the lighting schemes, video engineering, and more. And of course, they take advantage of various technologies in nearly every facet of television production, from scriptwriting to video editing. Similar technologies are also used in elective courses such as scriptwriting, introduction to media technology, and advanced media technology.

In addition to increasing their self-confidence, this program has allowed a growing number of these students to achieve eligibility for admission to post-secondary programs. This unique learning opportunity also provides the necessary skills for students who choose to pursue training and work in the entertainment industry. Former students' work has been accepted into the Sundance Film Festival (*Pipe Dreams*, 2003), and numerous students now have careers in television and film.

Scenarios Grades 9–12 (Ages 14–18)

Studies in Motion

Grade Levels: 9–12

Technology Standards: 1, 2, 3, 4, 6

Content Area: Mathematics (Physics)

Teacher: Ben Smith

School: Red Lion Area High School

Location: Red Lion, Pennsylvania, United States

Technology in Education Is Global

After reading the Alice Walker novel, The Color Purple, Peter Crooke's students at Harriton High School (Rosemont, Pennsylvania) create original digital movies and music to explore how people are affected by their environment and how people can shape their environment.

Students in Ben Smith's physics class study motion by using a variety of technologies to record, analyze, and share their experiments. The project begins with students using a digital camera to take related still shots and a camcorder to record some type of motion (such as shooting a basketball or driving a car). Once the photography is done, students import the video into a digital video editing suite and use video motion analysis software to capture, position, and time data from the motion clip. The data can then be plotted, viewed in a table, or exported into another program for further analysis.

Once their analysis is complete, students use concept-mapping software to explain their motion study. This file is also used as the basis of a Web site. Links to the video clip, still photographs, and other supporting documentation are added to the concept map, and the files are uploaded to the Internet for a class presentation and discussion. Following this, students comment on each other's work using a discussion board.

The availability of technology for this project makes it easier for students to work through a complex, multistep problem while interacting with their peers.

Development Team

ISTE NETS Refresh Project Leadership Team

Lynn Nolan, NETS Refresh Director and Sr. Director of Education Leadership	*ISTE*
Lajeane Thomas, NETS Director	*Louisiana Tech University*
David Barr, Consultant	*ISTE*
Leslie S. Conery, Deputy CEO	*ISTE*
Mila M. Fuller, Director of Strategic Initiatives	*ISTE*
Don Knezek, CEO	*ISTE*
Anita McAnear, Acquisitions Editor	*ISTE*
Carolyn Sykora, Project Manager	*ISTE*

ISTE Accreditation and Standards Committee

Lajeane Thomas, Chair	*Louisiana Tech University*
Sheryl Abshire	*Calcasieu Parish Public Schools*
David Barr	*ISTE Consultant*
Jill Brown	*Albuquerque Academy*
Phil East	*University of Northern Iowa*
Kathy Hayden	*California State University San Marcos*
Peggy Kelly	*California State University San Marcos*
Paul Reinhart	*Conneaut Elementary School*
Heidi Rogers	*Northwest Council for Computer Education (NCCE)*

ISTE NETS Refresh Stakeholders Advisory Council

Jill Abbott	*Schools Interoperability Framework Association*
Stephen Andrews	*Intel® Education*
Barbara Cambridge	*National Council of Teachers of English*
Karen Cator	*Apple Inc.*
Deb DeVries	*Pearson Education*
Anuja Dharkar	*Adobe Systems Inc.*
James Everett	*Bellingham High School*
Alan Farstrup	*International Reading Association*
Liz Hoffman	*American Council on the Teaching of Foreign Languages*
Margaret Honey	*Wireless Generation*
Sharnell Jackson	*Chicago Public Schools*
Paige Kuni	*Intel® Education*
Michal LeVasseur	*National Council for Geographic Education*
Tim Magner	*U.S. Department of Education*
Frank Owens	*National Science Teachers Association*
Andrea Prejean	*National Education Association*
Gayle Thieman	*National Council for Social Studies*
Carla Wade	*State Education Technology Directors Association*
Mary Ann Wolf	*State Education Technology Directors Association*

Contributing Author for This Booklet

Susan Brooks-Young